In the spirit ⋯⋯⋯⋯⋯⋯⋯⋯ l
this contemporary and irreverent guide to, well,
savoir faire.

The history of champagne is filled with
royalty, elegance, romance, and happy celebration.
Even today, a good bubbly is perhaps the most
festive and flattering beverage of all. Ever notice
how a mere *uncorking* sends a ripple of interest
throughout the room?

So we thought this clever guide to *social grace*
was a timely and appropriate third Freixenet
companion to good times.

Cheers and have fun!

FREIXENET USA
P.O. BOX 1949
SONOMA, CALIFORNIA 95476

Freixenet
Méthode Champenoise—CAVA—

OTHER TITLES FROM FREIXENET

The Freixenet Book of Toasts & Graces
The Freixenet New Year's Eve Companion

The titles above are available free from the address on the preceding page. (Please include $4.00 each for postage and handling. Good while supplies last.)

The
Freixenet
Social
Survival
Guide

TODD LYON

The author thanks Jennifer Reiley, wine salesperson for Slocum & Sons, Inc., for her generous expertise; ticket sales expert Joseph Ramos for his advice and consultation; and Catherine Lendler and Barbara Lyon for their party games know-how.

Copyright © 2000 by Random House, Inc.

Published by Clarkson Potter/Publishers, New York, New York. Member of the Crown Publishing Group.

Random House, Inc. New York, Toronto, London, Sydney, Auckland www.randomhouse.com

CLARKSON N. POTTER is a trademark and POTTER is a registered trademark of Random House, Inc.

Printed in Spain

Design by Jan Derevjanik

Illustrations by David Sanchez

ISBN 0-609-50344-8

10 9 8 7 6 5 4 3 2 1

First Edition

Contents

"Frame your mind to mirth and merriment,
which bars a thousand harms and lengthens life…"

WILLIAM SHAKESPEARE
The Taming of the Shrew

CHAPTER 1

The Perfect Guest

PARTY GUEST COMMANDMENTS

- **When in doubt, dress up.** You don't want to embarrass yourself by showing up in flannel and denim when everyone else is in suits and dresses. On the other hand, you should probably avoid tuxedos and sequins, unless specified on the invitation.

- **Don't assume** it's okay to bring friends, kids, or even a date. Make a phone call a few days in advance. Tell your hosts who you'd like to bring. If your request isn't immediately granted with open arms, you probably shouldn't go through with it.

- **Be 15 to 20 minutes late.** If it's a dinner party, and you're running 30 minutes or more behind schedule, call and alert your hosts. If it's a cocktail party and you're going to be more than an hour late, call with a good excuse and an ETA.

- **Introduce yourself** (and your date) to strangers. Engage them in conversation. Here's a no-fail approach: "Hi, I'm (your name). How do you know (your host)? I hope there's a crazy story attached to your first meeting. . . ."

- **Don't just sit there**—move around. If it's a casual affair with a self-serve bar, ask others if you can get them a drink before you refill your own. Approach loners and chat them up. Introduce people to each other.

- **Ask permission before smoking.** Say "Is there a designated smoking area?" instead of "May I smoke?" You might end up outside with other outcasts, but that can be fun if you keep your festive attitude intact.

- **Know your limits.** If tequila makes you crazy, don't drink it, even if it's a margarita party and there are seven different kinds being offered. Same goes for gin at martini parties, and so on. Even responsible drinkers sometimes go a bit too far; if this happens to you, ask your hosts for a cup of coffee, then switch to seltzer.

- **Know when it's time to go.** If the party is swinging way beyond the time stated on the invitation, be sensitive to your hosts' energy levels; pick up on unspoken signals such as glazed eyes and stifled yawns, and get yourself and your coat out the door before you become a burden.

- **Say thank you.** When you're leaving, it's essential that you seek out the party-givers and thank them before you go. Follow up with a phone call the next day or a nice note. (See page 15.)

- **Offer to help your host.** For small gatherings, and after the festivities wind down, ask your hosts if you can help straighten up. Your kind offer will be noted, but (lucky you) almost certainly refused.

WHAT WILL YOU BRING TO THE PARTY?

Good guests never arrive at a house party empty-handed. In addition to invisible gifts such as a sense of humor, a good appetite, and a willingness to participate in a round or two of Pass the Orange, he or she rings the doorbell bearing an offering to the party gods that will be enjoyed that very evening by the general party population.

NEVER-FAIL CLASSICS

- A bottle or two of sparkling wine or champagne (best of all)

- A box of prestige chocolates

- A bottle of your favorite wine

- An intriguing liqueur
- A six-pack of high-end beer or ale (in bottles, please)

INTERESTING ALTERNATIVES

- A toast, written by you, to be read at the perfect moment
- A CD that will thrill your hosts and inspire outbursts of spontaneous dancing
- A flowering houseplant, bonsai tree, or small potted palm
- A decorative candle (unscented, of course)
- A seasonal gift (Christmas tree ornament, pumpkins or gourds, Fourth of July sparklers, etc.)
- A box of good cigars
- A special nonalcoholic beverage such as locally made cider, Italian soda, or Jamaican ginger ale
- Something event-appropriate (for a tailgate party, bring pennants or pom-poms and pass them around; for a picnic, bring a watermelon or a package of rubber ants)

UNLESS THEY'RE REQUESTED IN ADVANCE, AVOID BRINGING

- Fresh flowers. Busy hosts don't want to stop what they're doing, find a vase, trim the stems, and make an arrangement on the spot—or find a place to put it.
- Party foods that need to be heated, assembled, or arranged on-site. If you bring unsolicited edibles to a dinner party, make sure they're simple to serve and won't interfere with the planned menu. Homemade (or expensive) cookies are fine, as are fancy nuts and the aforementioned chocolates, because they can be easily integrated into a dessert spread. For casual cocktail parties, you can confidently bring finger foods that are ready to serve (think shrimp

cocktail for 20, figs wrapped in prosciutto, spanking fresh sushi). Make sure your offering is ready to serve and presented on a throwaway platter. If you must use a plate of your own, discreetly tape your name to its bottom.

DON'T EVEN THINK ABOUT BRINGING

- Something that must be prominently displayed. Forget the herb wreath, the gingerbread house, the talking-tree centerpiece, or the life-size Hulk Hogan blow-up doll.

- A wrapped gift of a personal nature (unless it's your host's birthday or something), because it will make other guests feel inadequate—oafish, even. If you're the host and this happens to you, squirrel the gift away and open it at a later date.

- A pricey bottle of wine, champagne, or other potable that you want your host to put aside for an implicitly "more special" occasion.

A NOTE TO THE SUAVE

Party-givers appreciate unscheduled injections of fun. One hostess of our acquaintance recalls the night a guest brought an assortment of rubber teeth—Dracula teeth, monster teeth, Austin Powers teeth—and passed them out to dinner guests just before dessert. Cameras appeared, inhibitions vanished, and from that point on her party swung in a wonderful way. So if you have a game, video, toy, sight gag, anecdote, prop, or joke that can be enjoyed by everybody (including 80-year-old Aunt Cecilia), bring it along.

CONVERSATION STARTERS

It's natural to feel awkward, or even terrified, when facing a room full of strangers and people who look vaguely familiar (which is much worse, as any chronic name-forgetter will tell you). So it helps to have a few ready-made conversation starters in your bag of party tricks, in case your personality suddenly drops dead.

THE "WHERE AM I?" APPROACH

Walk up to somebody who looks like he or she may have a sense of humor and say, "I'm confused. Is this the Daughters of the American Revolution hoedown?" Or, "Is this the meeting of the Flat Earth Society?" You can also try Survivors of the *Titanic* Reunion, Adult Children of Adults wingding, etc.

THE CELEBRITY LOOK-ALIKE OPENER

"You look like Isabella Rossellini. Are you a movie star?" If you're using this opener, make sure the person you address really does resemble the celebrity you mention. Hopefully he or she will decide that you are absolutely marvelous and the only person in the room worth talking to.

THE REVERSE CELEBRITY LOOK-ALIKE OPENER

"Don't tell anyone, but I'm (fill in celebrity name here)." Think of the possibilities.

THE JEWELRY RUSE

This works best for women meeting other women, or gay men meeting women, and goes something like this: "Oh! That bracelet is divine. Is there a story behind it?" When she says that she spied it in a shop window in Paris, or she bought it on the internet, or she found it in the bushes out back, let that lead to other lines of communication, such as, "Oh, I've always wanted to go to Paris. What brought you there?"

WHEN ALL ELSE FAILS, TRY

"You don't look familiar but I think you ought to."

A NOTE TO THE SUAVE

Don't dominate one person's time. If a chat is going on a bit too long, excuse yourself by saying, "I'm sorry, can we keep talking in a little while? If I don't say hello to so-and-so right now, he'll never speak to me again." Of course, you can also just say, "I'm off like a prom dress."

OPENING LINES TO AVOID

"Is that your real hair?"

"You remind me of my mother."

"One more of those drinks and you'll be under the table. Two more and you'll be under the host. Hi, I'm your host."

"I suppose the old ride is out of the question." (This is an Irish expression, meaning, "You won't be sleeping with me tonight, will you?")

TIPS FOR REMEMBERING PEOPLE'S NAMES

Memory experts have tricks for remembering people's names, and they usually have to do with visual cues. Let's say you're introduced to a woman named Susan, who is wearing a blue dress. Make a little rhyme in your head like, "Sue in blue." You can make a whole room full of easy-to-remember characters who sound like refugees from a Batman movie: "Tall Paul," "Short Mort," "Chester the Molester," and so on.

Unfortunately, this trick can actually create confusion at big parties when you remember that Jeanne is in jeans . . . or was that Gene in jeans? Is "Red Ed" the guy with the red hair or the one with the red nose?

It's also true that most people plagued with poor name recall are much more embarrassed about forgetting the names of people they already know. If this describes you, then the best trick is to recruit your date (hopefully it's your spouse or somebody who knows you almost as well) to do the famous name game. Here it goes:

YOU: I'm so glad you're here! It's great to see you again. Have you met Tracy, my date? Tracy, this is the book collector I was telling you about.

TRACY: Glad to meet you. I'm sorry, I didn't catch your name. . . .

EMERGENCY PARTY ETIQUETTE

- When there's something awful in your mouth, like a piece of gristle or a bit of claw dredged up from the lobster bisque, put your fork in your mouth, deposit the piece on the tines, and return it to the side of your plate.

- When you take an hors d'oeuvre on a toothpick from a waiter's tray or a buffet table, don't put the toothpick back next to the uneaten food. There should be a small bowl or receptacle near the hors d'oeuvres for the discards; if not, wrap them in your cocktail napkin and put them in a waste-basket. As a last resort, stick them in your pocket or purse and throw them out later.

- To gracefully discard olive pits, see above.

- For spills and stains, see page 57, and don't let the host do all the dirty work.

THANK-YOU NOTES

When you were a child, your mother hounded you mercilessly until you wrote thank-you notes to each and every friend and relative who gave you a birthday gift. How could you let all that good nagging go to waste?

YOU ABSOLUTELY, POSITIVELY MUST WRITE A THANK-YOU NOTE

- When someone has given a party for you. Write a gushing letter of thanks to your hosts, and also to guests who helped plan the party and to people who gave you gifts, toasts, and testimonials. Include snapshots of the event, if you have them.

- After any formalized event such as a shower or wedding. For these events, it's de rigueur to have an inscribing angel who writes down who gave you what gift, which greatly helps in the note-writing department.

YOU REALLY SHOULD WRITE A THANK-YOU NOTE

- After a dinner party to which you and a small group of others were specifically invited in advance.

- After a fabulous bash that took a lot of effort on your host's part. If you had a blast, loved the food, and/or made new friends, include that information in the note.

- Following any event in which you were a "wild-card" candidate—that is, if you're new in town, or you're a significant other invited out of consideration for your mate, or if it's the first time one of your business friends has had you into his or her home.

- After one or more nights as a house guest, to thank your hosts for opening up their home.

A PHONE CALL WILL DO

- After an annual event, like a friend's New Year's Eve party that you've gone to for five years running.

- Following a spontaneous or very casual soirée.

YOU'RE OFF THE HOOK

- When the party was hosted by a corporation, restaurant, or nightclub. Ditto movie premieres, awards dinners (unless you won something—see Item #1), and any event to which you paid admission.

OFFICE PARTY DOS AND DON'TS

Office parties are not so much "parties" as they are business events with crepe paper. As such, they require an entirely different set of rules than real parties, which are designed to make you forget that you work in an office, or have a job at all.

- **Wear a suit.** No matter what you do for the company, whether you're CEO or a cafeteria worker, wear a dark suit. If it's a holiday party, men are allowed to wear a red tie, and women are allowed to wear a sparkly brooch.

- **Don't have fun.** If you find yourself in the corner, laughing uproariously with a client or coworker, immediately put down your drink, reapply your game face, and keep networking.

- **Don't get drunk.** Don't even get a teensy bit tipsy. If you must drink at all, have one glass of wine, or one cocktail, or two glasses of champagne, just to be a sport.

- **Don't eat.** You may nibble delicately at the buffet, but you mustn't load down your plate and park yourself at a table to chow down. In fact, don't sit at all.

- **No dancing.** Save that for the club you're sneaking out to later.

- **Don't talk about sex,** religion, politics, controversial topics, negative topics, or anything bad regarding your job, your coworkers, your boss, or the company in general. Your best bet is to politely listen and keep steering the conversation back to the other person's interests.

- **Stay for no more than 1.5 hours.** Thank your "host" and say what a lovely event it has been. There's no need to explain where you're going; if you're asked point-blank, just say, "I unfortunately have another engagement that I couldn't reschedule."

CHAPTER 2

The Perfect Host

PARTY HOST COMMANDMENTS

- **Be cheerful and pleasant at all times,** even if someone has just knocked over a candle and the tablecloth is on fire. It's your job to suffer fools gladly.

- **Greet guests at the door,** take their coats, and offer them a drink. After that, don't wait on them.

- **Keep circulating.** Avoid deep or lengthy conversations; move around and make sure that everyone is engaged and happy.

- **Introduce everybody to each other.** You're what they have in common, after all, so it's up to you to provide the link.

- **Keep the food and drinks coming.** When the cheese station is looking a little picked over, freshen it; keep the ice buckets full; wash some extra glasses if you're getting low; pass hors d'oeuvres when they're hot out of the oven.

- **Mind the music, and don't let it stop.** Lack of background music can be a real buzz kill. During the first few hours, play discs that won't overwhelm conversation; as the party gets hotter, turn up the volume a bit and switch to danceable tunes.

- **Have at least one planned activity.** This can be as simple as a toast to someone's birthday or as complicated as a full-gang game of Sardines (see page 26). In any case, it's important to have something for the entire group to get involved in, because it breaks up clusters and cliques, gives strangers something to talk about, and, in the case of Sardines, might cause half your guests to spend some quality time together under your bed.

- **Stay alert.** It's okay to have a celebratory cocktail or two, but it's up to you to be the most sober person at the party. Remember, you are the resident sobriety detector.

- **Deal discreetly with the inebriated.** When a guest goes overboard, take him or her aside and simply ask, "Are you driving?" If not, find out who that person's ride is and make sure the driver's in good shape. If the soused person thinks he or she can drive, you have three options: 1) Offer coffee, seltzer, and food, and wait 30 minutes. Sometimes this will bring a person right back to earth and clear their judgment regarding motor vehicle operation. 2) Find a ride for your guest. This is less obvious—and less embarrassing— than calling a cab. Arrange to have the guest's car delivered the next day. 3) Say "I would feel better if you lay down for 20 minutes." Settle the person in the guest room, and expect an overnight stay.

- **If children are invited,** be sure to plan ahead for these guests as well. Offer them kid-friendly party foods, a table of their own, and favors and games that promote non-messy fun.

THE ELEMENTS OF FUN: A PARTY-GIVER'S CHECKLIST

CONSUMABLES

____ Food. Chips, nuts, cheese, paté, olives, bread, crackers, herbed salami, a roasted turkey, a baked ham, a tray of sushi, a smoked salmon, a big bowl of shrimp, and a table of desserts will all be appreciated.

_____ Drink. Wine, beer, champagne, and/or liquor should be present in abundance, as well as mixers, sodas, and at least one interesting non-alcoholic beverage such as hot mulled cider.

_____ Ice. There's no such thing as too much ice. You'll need a half-pound of ice for each guest, plus lots more for coolers and champagne buckets.

_____ Coffee. Make a pot after midnight and set it out with cream, sugar, and artificial sweetener.

ATMOSPHERE

_____ Music. You don't have to hire a 15-piece mariachi band, but you must have a good stereo system and a fine selection of party CDs. If your collection isn't geared toward the festive, the silly, and the soul-train-line-inspiring, borrow discs from friends—or even have guests bring their favorites for a musical potluck.

_____ Lighting. Banish overhead lights. Keep lighting dim and indirect. Create dramatic pools of light in key areas by clustering choirs of candles together, balling up Christmas lights and setting them out in bowls, or installing a mirror ball (with pin spot). Black lights should be avoided, because they instantly reveal who has fake teeth and who's wearing a white bra under her sweater. If you have a fireplace, light a roaring fire to inject any party with relaxed elegance.

_____ Decorations. You don't need piles of balloons or miles of crepe paper, unless you're hosting a high school prom. But it's nice to have flowers, candles, and event-appropriate visuals, such as a big "Happy Birthday, You Old Fossil" banner.

ESSENTIAL EQUIPMENT

_____ Paper goods. Buy cups, heavy-gauge plates, and napkins in various sizes, and don't forget the forks and knives. Even if you're using your own glassware and tableware, you should have stacks of cocktail napkins on hand for use as coasters, Frito grease blotters, spill-wipers, and olive pit receptacles.

_____ Ashtrays. Even if you're banishing smokers to the back porch, have plenty of these on hand.

_____ Beer cooler. An antique copper kettle is the most attractive option. A galvanized aluminum garbage can isn't as pretty, but if you line it with a heavy-duty garbage bag it will get the job done. The ugliest of all are those plastic coolers that get hauled around to football games.

_____ And don't forget . . . corkscrews, bottle openers, stirrers, cocktail shakers, ice bucket and tongs, cutting boards, and enough sharp knives to handle meats and cheeses at the buffet and lemons and limes at the bar.

INVITATION DOS AND DON'TS

Phoning and faxing are for lazy hosts. The really good ones send out invitations—fun, original invitations that set the tone for the party and inspire and delight the invited. Here's how to create the best party invitations ever.

Do make your invitation personal. Put a photo montage together that includes you, your dog, your best friends—maybe with their heads superimposed on magazine bodies. Or, take a plain white card and cover it with your own lipstick kisses (unless you're worried about mailing your DNA all over town). You can handwrite invitations on coasters, tell the story with rubber stamps, play with gold leafing, create something fancy on your computer . . . anything but preprinted, store-bought invites.

Don't enclose sparkles or confetti in the envelopes. This was cute 10 years ago; now it's just annoying.

Do worry about paper, print, and design quality if you're hosting a formal or semiformal event. No scrimping.

Don't worry about paper, print, and design quality if you're throwing a wingding, a rave, or a smash-up.

Do state clearly on the invitation whether kids are welcome or not. If you want them, invite them; if you don't, include the words "adults only, please."

Don't wait too long to get to the post office. Invitations should be mailed a month to two weeks before an event; those that arrive too close to the date can be perceived as "unvitations" and will guarantee a sparse turnout.

Do find festive postage. People tend to be more excited by envelopes bearing disco dancers or George Gershwin than those with Herbert Hoover or Thomas Jefferson (although he was quite a party boy, we hear).

Don't be too upset if people don't RSVP in time—or at all. Yes, it's rude and inconvenient, but it's common; studies show that 30 to 40 percent of people don't respond as they should.

INVITATION CHECKLIST

____ Day of week, date, year

____ Time party begins, time party ends

____ Type of party (barbecue, birthday party, dinner party, etc.)

____ How to dress (casual, black-tie optional, cocktail garb, etc.)

____ Address

____ Directions (these can be included on a separate sheet)

____ Special instructions (no gifts, adults only, parking instructions, etc.)

____ Phone number, fax number, e-mail address

____ Your name as well as that of any other host(s)

A NOTE TO THE SUAVE

If you're throwing a party in a big city, give a taxi/subway-friendly address that includes cross streets, such as "39 East 19th Street, between Park and Broadway."

THE BASIC PARTY BAR

Your bar doesn't have to be swank or expansive. It just needs to be well-stocked and efficient enough to keep your guests wet. Whether someone's tending bar or the whole setup is self-serve, you'll need:

- **Bottled beer,** in coolers
- **Sparkling wine,** in coolers or champagne buckets
- **Red wine**

- **White wine,** in coolers or champagne buckets
- **Liquor.** If 90 percent of your cocktailing friends prefer vodka, and the other 10 percent drink scotch, you know what to buy. If preferences are a mystery, provide vodka, gin, rum, scotch, bourbon, tequila, and dry vermouth (if martinis are to be made).
- **Mixers.** Tonic, club soda, plain seltzer, spring water, cranberry juice and orange juice should do it. Pineapple or tomato juice can also be a welcome surprise.
- **Sodas.** Cola, diet cola, lemon/lime soda, and flavored seltzers are all useful.
- **Fruit.** Stock up on lemons, limes, lemon twists, and green olives (without pimientos, if you're making grown-up martinis).
- **Equipment.** Corkscrew, bottle opener, knife, cutting board, stirrer (or long spoon), and a cocktail shaker with a strainer are the minimum requirements.
- **Glassware.** If you've got the proper glass for every drink, congratulations, and would you please invite me to your next party? On the other hand, if you're merely mortal and are forced to use plastic, buy two sizes: large 8-ounce cups for beer and sodas, and smaller cups of about 6 ounces for wine and cocktails. Figure three vessels per guest.
- **Cocktail napkins.** Stacks and stacks.
- **Ice bucket and tongs.** Your friends may love you, but it doesn't mean they want your hands on their ice.

A NOTE TO THE SUAVE

Set your bar up where it won't create a bottleneck. Keep it away from doorways—especially the entrance—and for God's sake, don't put it in the kitchen, which is guaranteed to be jammed with people, even without the presence of booze.

NO-FAIL PARTY GAMES

Think you're too cool for party games? Here are five games beyond charades and twenty questions that will change your mind.

SARDINES
Turn off the lights. Elect someone "it," and instruct him or her to hide somewhere in the house while everyone else counts to 100 ("one can of sardines, two cans of sardines . . ."). At 100, guests scramble to find "it." Once a guest finds the hidden person, he or she remains silent and hides next to "it." Eventually, 90 percent of the search party will be squeezed into one hiding place, which is how the game got its name. The first person to have found "it" becomes "it" during the next round—if you can bear that much togetherness a second time.

WELL, I NEVER
Taking turns (either around the room or spontaneously), each person names something he or she has never experienced, for instance, "I've never been to Vegas." If everybody else in the room has been, the player earns one point. If one or more players have also never been to Vegas, no points are scored. This game can be quite revealing; a friend who recently played it learned that one of her friends couldn't swim, and that two of her particularly erudite party guests never graduated from high school.

HAT TRICKS

Ask every player to silently write down, on slips of paper, the names of 10 famous people, fictional characters, animals, mythical heroes, and so on. Put all the names in a hat and mix them up. Pass the hat to the person on your left, and set a kitchen timer for 2 minutes. That person must draw names, one at a time, and quickly give spoken or body language clues to the person on his or her left. Example: If the name is "Dudley Do-Right," the sender might say, "He's a cartoon character, a Canadian Mountie, he's in love with his horse. . . ." When the receiver correctly gives the answer, the sender draws another name from the hat and starts giving clues again. The host's job is to write down the number of correct answers given within 2 minutes. The team with the highest score wins.

MURDER

Place slips of paper in a hat or a bowl, one for each guest. All slips will be blank except for one—this has an "M" written on it. The person who draws it is the murderer, a fact he or she must keep quiet. The murderer's job is to "kill" people by winking at them, without letting anyone else see them do it. Conversation will resume, people will keep eating dessert or whatever, but once they're winked at they're "dead"—out of the game. The game ends after everyone's been killed or when a still-living player sees the murderer killing someone else and makes an arrest.

POET'S CORNER

Each player is given a pen and a piece of paper and instructed to write a line of poetry across the top. It can be original or robbed from a famous poem, a song lyric, or even an ad slogan. Writers then pass their papers to the person on their left. Each person adds a line (rhyming or not) to their new poem, then folds the paper down so that the first line is hidden. The "poems" go around the table, with only one line showing at a time, until everyone has written at least one line per page (or until you run out of space on the paper). Each writer then takes a turn unfolding his or her communal poem and reading it aloud—hopefully to uncontrolled laughter on the part of the coauthors.

CHAPTER 3

Around the Table

FORMAL DINING
WITHOUT FEAR

You're seated at an excruciatingly correct table, faced
with an army of glassware, a confusing nest of plates,
and more silverware than you know what to do with.
Don't fake an asthma attack and run from the room:
virtually every table setting in the Western world,
from roadhouse plain to White House fancy, follows
the same basic rules. Learn them and you will forever
dine without embarrassment.

- Your napkin is located on your plate or to the
  extreme left of your place setting. Immediately
  pick it up, unfold it, and place it in your lap. Resist
  the temptation to put it on your head à la Laverne
  and Shirley, even if it's folded into a shape that
  looks an awful lot like a party hat.

- Glassware, which may include a water goblet, a
  champagne flute, and white wine, red wine, and
  liqueur glasses, is placed to the right of your plate.
  Don't worry about them: they will be filled with
  appropriate beverages, at appropriate times, as the
  meal unfolds.

- There may be a large plate at your place when you
  sit down. This is probably not a dinner plate but
  something called a "charger," which is sometimes
  placed under the dinner plate or bread plate, or
  taken away when the first course is served. Your
  bread plate is the significantly smaller dish to your
  left. Use that for your bread needs.

- You'll note that forks are on the left side of the
  plate, while spoons and knives are on the right.
  Each utensil has a job, and the widely accepted
  rule is to work from the outside in. If you start with
  a soup course, for instance, you'll find your soup

spoon at the extreme right of your setting. If a salad comes next, look for your salad fork (shorter tines than a dinner fork) on the far left. When each course is finished, its designated silverware is also cleared away.

- Some courses arrive with their own utensils. Sorbet, for instance, which refreshes the palate between courses, is usually served with a small spoon.

- Dessert forks, teaspoons, and teacups are often set after the flotsam and jetsam of dinner has been cleared away. However, some formal settings have the dessert fork and teaspoon positioned above the plate throughout the duration of the meal.

- Finger bowls are increasingly rare these days, but still make appearances after particularly messy entrées such as steamed lobster. Take note: if a wee bowl of water, with or without a floating lemon slice, is placed before you, *don't drink it*. Delicately dip your fingertips in it, then dry them off with your napkin.

- When in doubt, follow the leader—that is, your host and/or hostess. If you do what they do, you'll always be correct, whether it's rule book–perfect or not.

THE SECRET LANGUAGE OF UTENSILS

You're not done yet: forks, knives, and even napkins have their own code of etiquette.

- If you need to leave the table in the middle of a course—or if you pause to hear a speech or a story—place your fork and knife on your plate in an inverted V, with the fork tines facedown. This is a signal to the server that you're not finished eating.

- When you've had your fill and are ready to have your place cleared, lay your knife across the right-hand rim of the plate (cutting side in), with your fork by its side (nearer the center of the plate).

- If you get up from the table mid-meal, do not put your napkin on the table. Put it, rumpled and unfolded, on the seat of your chair. This is not a secret signal; it simply spares other guests from having to look at your soiled linen while they're trying to eat.

- When dinner is over and everyone is getting up to leave, you can drop your napkin on the table.

TABLE MANNERS
(WITH OR WITHOUT TABLES)

- If seating is limited, think *Titanic* and let women and children sit first.

- Upon being seated, immediately put your napkin in your lap.

- Elbows off the table. And sit up straight.

- If olive oil is served with bread, decant a small amount onto your bread plate. Then tear off a small piece of bread and dredge it just before eating it.

- If a communal dish of butter is circulated, use the butter knife to transfer a small amount onto your bread plate, not onto the bread itself. Then tear off a small piece of the bread. Butter and eat.

- Confused by the menu? Ask your server for help. It's okay if you don't know that *tilapia* is a whitefish or that *carpaccio* is raw beef, and it's much better to find out first than to make a deadly ordering mistake.

- If you have food allergies, mention them before ordering.

- Soup is spooned away from yourself.

- With the exception of the bread at the start of a meal, which is there to ward off starvation, don't begin eating until everyone has been served. Ignore this rule if you're at a barbecue, a buffet, or any event where food is served in waves—when it's hot off the grill, for instance.

- Americans usually "switch forks"—that is, they put down their knives and transfer their forks to the right hand after cutting meat. But it's perfectly acceptable to eat "Continental style," in which the knife stays in the right hand and the fork in the left.

- When presented with a lemon wedge to squeeze on your shellfish (or whatever), stick a small cocktail fork in the side of the wedge and twist it. This keeps juice-spewing down to a minimum.

- When eating skewered dishes (shish kebab, satay), slide all the food off the skewer before digging in.

- If you're sharing dessert—or sharing tastes of others' entrées—place the "tastes" on your bread or dinner plate, not directly into your mouth.

FOODS YOU CAN EAT WITH YOUR HANDS

Barbecued ribs

Sandwiches (hamburgers, hot dogs, tacos, etc.)

Wings

Corn on the cob

French fries

Potato chips (or any chips)

Hors d'oeuvres

Sushi (if you can't manage chopsticks)

Pizza (only by the slice; personal pizzas require a knife and fork)

Raw clams and oysters

Shrimp cocktail

Antipasti (celery, olives, cheese, etc.)

Lobster or crab that's been steamed in its shell

Steamed artichokes

Steamed asparagus spears (unsauced)

Grapes (unless you're in England)

Ethiopian food

FOODS YOU CAN EAT WITH YOUR HANDS ONLY IF YOU'RE OUTDOORS

Chicken (by the piece)

Watermelon (by the slice)

RESTAURANTLY BEHAVIOR

OR, HOW NOT TO MAKE A FOOL OF YOURSELF WHILE DINING OUT

- Don't wear a cap or, if you're a man, a hat of any kind.

- Don't wear a T-shirt, even if it's summer and blazing hot outside. (Women can get away with heavy-gauge T-shirts, as long as there isn't any writing on them.)

- Don't put your napkin around your neck. Keep it in your lap.

- Don't saw your dinner roll in half and make a butter sandwich.

- If you need to send something back to the kitchen —if your steak is undercooked or there's a hair in your grilled veggies—don't make a big deal of it, and don't announce it to the rest of the table. Quietly confer with your waitperson and resolve the problem.

- Summon your waitperson subtly, with eye contact and body language. Don't wave your arm or call out—unless you *want* to be ignored.

- Don't talk on your cell phone. If you absolutely must make a call, go to a private spot (the rest room comes to mind).

- Don't sneeze at the table (if you can help it), and don't blow your nose. Excuse yourself and make for the rest room.

- Avoid blotting your lipstick on linen napkins. Don't pat your lips, wipe around them.

When awful things happen to good people in restaurants, the best ones laugh it off. Example: A close friend, in the middle of a business luncheon, had an entire bottle of ketchup poured on her head. It happened when a passing waiter knocked the bottle off his tray and caught it midair. The cap flew off, its contents were airborne, and . . . well, you know the rest. Our red-faced (literally) heroine swiftly disappeared into the ladies' room, where she managed to make herself presentable with the help of water and the hand dryer. She returned triumphant, took a bow, and thus impressed her colleagues—who were all treated to a free lunch.

HOW TO GET A GOOD TABLE IN A RESTAURANT

- It pays to have a "favorite" restaurant and to remember the maître d's name.

- Call well in advance to make reservations.

- Request a table at a window, near the door, or in a romantic spot.

- When asked to leave your name, put "Doctor," "Judge," or "Chef" in front of it, or "Esquire" after it. Certain friends of ours always make reservations as "Dr. and Mrs. No," and claim they inevitably get the best seats in the house.

- If, on the day of the dinner, you're seated in horrible seats so close to the kitchen that you need hair nets, or so close to the bathroom that you need gas masks, speak to the maître d'. Explain that you (a doctor! a lawyer! a judge! a chef!) are celebrating a special event and need a better table.

- If you're willing to wait at the bar, an understanding maître d' can improve your chances of getting a better table.

- If that doesn't work, slip the fellow a ten . . . or a twenty in dire emergencies.

PICKING UP THE CHECK

- The person who made the date (or called the meeting) is the one who pays.

- If someone else insists on paying, and he or she is a "senior" person at the table (a boss, a parent, a multimillionaire), don't fight it too hard. Let it happen and give thanks.

- If dinner is a group affair with a bunch of friends, split the check evenly between individuals or couples. If you ordered the lobster or had an expensive glass of grappa at the end of the meal, put in more or hand the extra money to the person who ordered the chicken and didn't drink.

- It's perfectly okay to have a waitperson split a check between two credit cards. Any more than two is too much to ask. Having cash on hand is always appreciated.

A HINT TO THE HEROIC

If you're taking friends out and absolutely want to pay, give your credit card to your waitperson—in private—at the beginning of the meal. When the last cup of coffee has been ordered, slip away to the bar or wait station and take care of the bill.

CHAPTER 4

Cheers

THE NEOPHYTE'S GUIDE TO ORDERING WINE

There's a first time for everything. If you've shied away from ordering and tasting wine in a fine restaurant, you're in for a treat. It's a wonderful ritual, because it puts you in the position of ushering in the pleasures of the grape to your lucky dinner companions. The following is a basic guide to which wines complement which foods. Of course, the only real rule is to drink what you like; eventually you'll develop your own inner wine list.

CHAMPAGNE OR SPARKLING WINES

Perhaps the most versatile wines of all, they make great aperitifs, and the refreshing, palate-cleansing effect complements spicy, fried, salty, or ethnic foods. Sparkling wine varies in sweetness and is thus appropriate for different courses.

- **Brut:** Very dry, best with hors d'oeuvres, appetizers, or fish, shellfish, and chicken dishes. (Champagne and lobster is a fab combination.)
- **Extra dry:** Slightly sweeter than brut; order with the above, to accompany dessert, or simply to celebrate.
- **Sec, demi-sec, doux:** Very sweet champagnes, usually reserved for dessert courses only.

BIG REDS

Great with steak, hearty beef, and pork dishes.
- *Bordeaux* • *Cabernet Sauvignon* • *Rhone reds*
- *Syrah (or Shiraz)* • *Zinfandel*

MEDIUM OR SOFT REDS

Pair with lamb, veal dishes, lighter pork dishes such as tenderloin, and red-sauced pasta.

- *Merlot* • *Chianti and other Italian reds* • *Burgundy*
- *French Pinot Noir* • *Rioja*

LIGHT REDS

Excellent with the above meats plus roasted duck, turkey, chicken, and salmon and tuna steaks.

- *Beaujolais* • *California Pinot Noir*

ROSÉ

Whether still or sparkling, try it as an aperitif or with light chicken dishes, main-course salads, omelets, and Mexican or spicy foods.

BIG WHITES

Order with poultry, pasta, fish steaks, and the lightest veal dishes.

- *White Burgundy* • *California Chardonnays*

MEDIUM WHITES

Great with poultry, fish, shellfish, and pasta dishes with clear or white sauces.

- *Chardonnay* • *Chablis* • *Sauvignon Blanc (Loire Valley)*
- *White Bordeaux* • *New Zealand whites* • *Pinot Blanc*

SAVORY OR LIGHT WHITES

Best for delicate fish dishes, vegetarian dishes, or Pacific Rim cuisine.

- *Riesling* • *Pinot Grigio and other Italian whites*
- *White Zinfandel* • *Albariño and other Spanish whites*
- *Gewürztraminer*

AND KEEP IN MIND

Simple wines go best with complex foods; simple foods go best with complex wines. Thus, a basic grilled steak is perfectly accompanied by a Bordeaux that's full of age and interesting flavors. Conversely, if you're dining on a complicated curried chicken, go with an easy white like Chablis. If you're ordering wine for a table of pals whose orders range from broiled fish to stuffed pork chops, stick with Beaujolais or other light red. Champage is always a festive and versatile beginning to any meal.

HOW TO HOLD A WINE GLASS

By the stem. Always by the stem. If you hold it by the bowl, cold white wines, champagnes, and martinis will lose their chill, while cellar-temperature reds will become too warm.

WINE STEWARD ETIQUETTE

- After you've ordered, your server will bring your bottle to the table and show you the label to ensure that it is the wine you ordered. Pay attention: it's easy for wines to get mixed up because they're often retrieved by bin number, not by name. Also note if the wine level is more than an inch or so below the cork. If so, it's likely that the cork is defective, in which case you should mention the "low fill" to the wine steward.

- Once you've approved the selection, your server will open it for you and offer you the cork to examine. Don't sniff it: just make sure it doesn't look horribly dried out or moldy.

- Next, the server will pour a small amount of the wine into your glass. Holding it by the stem, and keeping the glass in contact with the table, swirl the wine a little bit. Take a sip, hold the wine in your mouth for a moment, purse your lips, and inhale gently. You should experience an intense— and hopefully pleasant—aroma. Slosh the wine around in your mouth and explore its flavors (this is called "chewing") before swallowing.

- After the wine has passed your inspection, the server will pour it into your and your dinner companions' glasses until they're about half-full.

- This process should be repeated with every bottle you order, even if you order the same wine.

A NOTE TO THE SUAVE

Don't be afraid to ask the steward for a suggestion. It might be a learning experience for you, and he knows the list and menu better than you will.

WHEN TO SEND A WINE BACK

Two bad things can happen to wines as they lay innocently in the cellar: 1) Air can seep through the cork, which will make the wine taste like either sherry or vinegar. You'll know this has happened if the wine seems like it should be poured on a salad, or if it tastes too strong, or, in the case of red wines, if it has turned slightly amber in color. 2) The cork can become infested with bacteria, causing the wine to take on an intensely moldy flavor. If you suspect that either of these phenomena have occurred, but aren't quite sure, ask your server to take a sip. Be assured that it's not bad form to return a bottle that's around the bend. After all, that's why wines are tasted in the first place.

TIME-HONORED TOASTS

Champagne for my true friends. True pain for my sham friends. [1]

Here's to champagne, the drink divine,
That makes us forget all our troubles;
It's made from a dollar's worth of wine,
And ten dollars' worth of bubbles. [2]

May our house always be too small to hold all our friends. [2]

Here's to eyes in your head and none in your spuds. [2]

To the holidays—all 365 of them. [2]

May the voices in your head always give you compliments.

QUOTES SUITABLE AS TOASTS

Early to rise and early to bed makes a man healthy, wealthy and dead.

—JAMES THURBER [2]

Home is where the wine is.

—MICHAEL CAINE [1]

I don't say we all ought to misbehave, but we ought to look as if we could.

—ORSON WELLES [3]

Anyone can sympathize with the sufferings of a friend, but it requires a very fine nature to sympathize with a friend's success.

—OSCAR WILDE [3]

1. *Wine Spectator's Champagne,* M. Shanken Communications, Inc., Running Press, Philadelphia, 1999.
2. Paul Dickson, *Toasts,* Crown Publishers, New York, 1991.
3. *The Dictionary of Humorous Quotations,* Evan Esar, ed., Dorset Press, New York, 1949.

Wine is light held together by moisture.
　　　　　　　—GALILEO [1]

There is but one pleasure in life equal to that of being called on to make an after-dinner speech, and that is not be called on to make one.
　　　　　　　—CHARLES DUDLEY WARNER [3]

Nothing succeeds like excess.
　　　　　　　—OSCAR WILDE [3]

A NOTE TO THE SUAVE

> *Never drink to your own toast—that is, when you're the one being toasted. It's equivalent to giving yourself a pat on the back.*

GREAT OPENINGS

Whether it's a prestige selection from an ancient winery or a young, punky blend from a place you've never heard of, you should give every bottle of champagne and wine an opening that even a seasoned sommelier would approve of.

HOW TO OPEN A BOTTLE OF SPARKLING WINE

Make sure the champagne bottle has been stored on its side and hasn't been jostled around recently. Check the temperature: it should feel like it just came out of the refrigerator (about 45° F.). If it's a bit tepid, put it on ice in a champagne bucket for 20 minutes.

1. Keep the bottle pointed away from every living creature, including yourself.

2. Prop the bottle on a table or countertop.

3. Remove the foil wrapper from the top part of the neck area.

4. Cover the top of the bottle with a cloth (a linen napkin or hand towel will do just fine).

5. While keeping the cork stabilized with one hand, loosen but don't remove the metal cage that holds the cork in place. This is done by untwisting the protruding wire loop. Never leave the cork unattended with the wire cage off.

6. Grasp the cork firmly. Hold the bottle from the base with your thumb inside the well and slowly twist it out from under the cork. Though you may hear a muffled pop, the bottle will more likely let out a gentle sigh when the deed is done.

7. Use a slow hand when decanting the bubbly into champagne flutes. Tilting the glass while pouring will help keep it from foaming up, but a slow, steady, trickle-like pour is the best strategy.

A NOTE TO THE SUAVE

Use narrow flutes or slightly flared tulip glasses when serving champagne. And don't chill the stemware. Sparkling wine is at its friskiest when served in cool, dry glasses.

HOW TO OPEN A BOTTLE OF WINE

Remember that reds should be served slightly cooler than room temperature, and whites must be served chilled (not frigid).

1. Use a good-quality jackknife corkscrew (aka "waiter's corkscrew")—the choice of professionals.

2. With the knife, score the foil around the neck of the bottle. Remove the resulting foil "cap" to expose the top of the cork. Never skip this step; a good percentage of bottle necks are clad in lead foil. If you plunge a corkscrew directly through the foil, you might introduce traces of lead into the wine.

3. Tuck the knife back into its slot and position the handle perpendicular to the corkscrew so it's shaped like a T. Hold the bottle at an angle, center the tip of the corkscrew on the cork, and twist it until the curved part of the corkscrew disappears.

4. Flip the handle down on one side and place the metal "foot" (looks like a bottle opener) on the edge of the bottle's rim, then pull the handle back up, so that it acts as a lever. The cork should release with ease. If it doesn't come out completely, just give the handle a quick upward tug.

5. If the cork breaks, gently reinsert the corkscrew into a solid portion of the remaining fragment and tease it out. Only as a last resort should you push the remaining cork into the bottle. If you're forced to take this drastic measure, use a strainer when pouring the wine (a coffee filter will do in a pinch).

6. Some wines, especially certain reds, need a good 15 minutes to "breathe" before being poured.

FOUR PERFECT CHAMPAGNE COCKTAILS WITH A PUNCH

The following brilliant concoctions should be prepared in the most elegant champagne flutes you can afford and served with a sly grin.

RITZ FIZZ

Freixenet, chilled
1 dash lemon juice
1 dash blue curaçao
1 dash nut liqueur
Lemon peel

Fill champagne flute with Freixenet. Add remaining ingredients and stir. Garnish with a lemon twist.

CHAMPAGNE COCKTAIL

1 sugar cube
3 dashes Angostura bitters
½ ounce brandy
3 ounces Freixenet, chilled
Orange slice
Cherry

In a champagne glass, combine sugar cube, bitters, and brandy. While stirring, add Freixenet. Garnish with orange slice and cherry.

BELLINI

2 to 3 ounces fresh peaches, peeled
4 to 5 ounces Freixenet, chilled
1 kiwi fruit, quartered

In a blender, puree peaches. Pour 4 to 5 ounces of juice into champagne glass. Add Freixenet and stir gently. Garnish with a wedge of kiwi fruit.

OCEAN BREEZE

Ice
2 ounces cranberry juice cocktail
2 ounces grapefruit juice
4 ounces Freixenet, chilled
Lime

Fill a champagne or highball glass with ice and pour in juices. Top with Freixenet and stir gently. Garnish with a lime twist.

CLASSIC CHAMPAGNE PUNCH

3 cups seasonal fruits, such as peeled oranges, strawberries,
  pineapple, sliced lemon, or apricots
16 to 18 ounces cognac
1 large block of ice
3 bottles of Freixenet, chilled
24 ounces sparkling water or club soda
Splash of maraschino cherry juice, if desired

When ready to serve, place the fruit in a large punch bowl and add the cognac. Add the ice and pour the Freixenet and sparkling water over it. Stir briefly, taking care not to flatten the bubbles. Add a splash of maraschino cherry juice, if you wish.

YIELD: 25 TO 30 SERVINGS

CHAPTER 5

Out on the Town

PARTY-CRASHING 101

Before learning the fine art of party-crashing, it's important to know when to crash and when not to crash.

- **Don't** crash house parties to which you were clearly not invited.

- **Do** crash house parties to which you weren't invited because nobody knew you were back in town.

- **Don't** crash charity events, you awful creature.

- **Definitely** crash gallery openings, film premieres, club parties, record release parties, and launch parties hosted by cosmetics, software, or sportswear companies.

HERE'S HOW TO CRASH A PARTY

- First of all, dress appropriately. If it's an opening, wear something black and subtly elegant.

- For big events, make friends with a bunch of ticket-holders and herd in with them.

- Ask the doorman if your name is on "the list." It won't be. Explain that there must be a mistake, and you've traveled a long way, and you're meeting your friends inside, and would he please make an exception? Be extra-nice and polite; doormen appreciate that.

- For premieres, release parties, and corporate launches, bring your business card and say you're a client or a provider, or say that your company worked on the event or your law firm represents the group in question.

Back in the high-flying '80s, a New York City friend heard that there was a huge party being held at the Museum of Natural History for Michael Jackson, who had just released his Thriller *album (remember that?). There were no tickets to be had and security was tight. Our friend dressed up, took the subway, and found an idle limo parked just outside the cordoned-off museum. She bribed the driver $20 to drive her two blocks to the grand entrance. When she arrived, bulbs flashed and uniformed doormen ushered her across the red carpet, and nobody even asked to see her invitation.*

Swing crooner and professional party boy Jaymes Bee wanted desperately to get into a record industry party to which he felt he should have been invited. So he got a costume designer friend to make him a hobo outfit, complete with cigarette butts and crushed cans hanging off his jacket and a garbage bag slung over his shoulder. Around his neck he wore a sign that said NOT INVITED. The press loved it and shot a lot of footage. Eventually someone in charge came out and let him in. In the garbage bag was a pressed tux. He changed into it and landed himself a record contract that night.

FROM WORK TO PLAY:
18 HOURS OF STYLE

If you're working "from nine to wine" and plan on socializing after hours, it helps to have outfits that can convert from buttoned-up to relaxed or from drab to fancy.

WOMEN

- Headed to a club or bar after work? Wear a pants suit or skirt suit with a slinky blouse underneath. Later, ditch the jacket.

- If you're attending a dress-up event after hours, wear a simple dress by day and accessorize it with earrings, bracelets, and dark lipstick by night. If you have a strand of pearls with a decorative clasp in back, wear the pearls to work, then turn them around and let the clasp sparkle out front.

- Pack your going-out essentials into a small purse or evening bag and put everything else in a briefcase. Leave the briefcase under your desk until the next day (you won't need it, trust me).

MEN

- Wear a groovy T-shirt under your Brooks Brothers shirt. Remove your shirt and tie before going out and wear just your T-shirt with your suit.

- In cooler weather, pack a sweater in your briefcase and trade your suit jacket for it when headed to a casual joint.

- Leave your briefcase at the office.

- Business suits work fine at semiformal events. Just remember to wear your best coat, leather gloves, cashmere scarf, and other evening-worthy outer-wear.

HOW TO LOOK PERFECTLY TOGETHER AT WORK EVEN IF YOU DIDN'T GO HOME LAST NIGHT

We won't ask *why* you didn't go home last night. Perhaps you had a deadline and worked until 4 A.M. at your desk, then fell asleep on the office sofa. Or, perhaps you were very naughty and suddenly realized, in the middle of a smoky poker game in the back room of a bar, that it was 6:30 A.M. and your meeting was starting in an hour. In any case, you need more than black coffee to get your rumpled, smelly self together.

- Buy new clothes. Find an open store, buy a new shirt, blouse, dress, socks, whatever, and change in the dressing room. Men might be able to get away with just a new tie and some underwear; unfortunately, most retail clothing stores don't open until 10 A.M.

- Borrow clothes from a coworker. This is a matter of making a panicked phone call to a friend at work who wears a similar size. Get him or her to grab something and meet you in the first-floor rest room.

- Hang your clothes in the shower. Not *in* the shower, but in the bathroom while you take a shower. This will at least remove major wrinkles as well as some telltale smells.

- Buy basic toiletries. Even the most primitive bathrooms have soap, paper towels, and toilet paper. Supplement this with cheap versions of whatever you need (toothbrush, comb) to look and feel like yourself.

- Improvise. It's amazing what you can do with common household items—many of which can also be found in kitchens of well-stocked offices.

Vaseline petroleum jelly: Removes makeup, moisturizes face, shines shoes.

Baking soda: Use straight from the box as toothpaste; mix with warm water as mouthwash; sprinkle under arms as deodorant.

Nonfat dry milk: Mix a teaspoon with warm water to remove makeup.

Tea bags: Soak in lukewarm water and place over eyes for 15 minutes to relieve puffiness.

Reddi Wip dessert topping: Doubles as shaving cream (wet skin first). And also removes makeup.

White vinegar: Cleans dentures and bridgework.

Vodka: Cleans eyeglasses.

Alka-Seltzer antacid: Relieves hangovers.

HOW TO TIE A BOW TIE

If you've ever tried to do this on your own, you know why people get married and stay together for the rest of their lives.

1. Wrap the tie around the outside of your flipped-up collar and adjust it so that the left side is about an inch and a half longer than the right.
2. Cross the long end over the short, and bring the long end through the center at the neck.

3. Fold the short end in half, crossing left, and hold it horizontally between collar points. Drape the long end in front.

4. Take the tip of the long end and loop it behind the center intersection.

5. Fold the remaining loose fabric in half and push it through the center knot.

6. Bring your collar down, then tighten the knot by adjusting the ends of both loops.

7. Most people put the tips of the collar behind the bow, but either style is acceptable.

A NOTE TO THE SUAVE

Wearing a cummerbund with that tie? Make sure the pleats are facing north.

THE WELL-PACKED EVENING BAG

Have you ditched your bulbous, straining, work-a-day pocketbook for a gorgeous little jeweled clutch? Excellent. Freud never sleeps, you know. Now: what will you pack inside that glittering euphemism you call an evening bag? We asked seasoned dating veterans, who know that big fun can be found in small purses. Their suggestions:

- **Cash.** Enough to take a long cab ride home, not enough to bail your date out of jail.

- **Identification.** A driver's license can be your best friend in any number of complicated situations. We won't mention them here.

- **Keys.** Edit your 3-pound clutch of brass down to the minimum requirements: house keys, safety deposit box key, key to your heart.

- **Makeup.** Carry only the essentials: foundation, concealer, powder, lipstick, eyeliner, mascara, a mirror, and something to sweep away melted makeup from under your eyes at 3 A.M.

- **Tissues.** There's a reason why your mother always had these stuffed up her sleeve: they're good for all kinds of untidy moments, from wiping lipstick off your date's shirt to dabbing tears from your eyes after laughing till it hurts.

- **Hairbrush, comb, styling products.** Making out in the back of a limo is delightful, but do you have any idea what it does to your *hair*? Don't leave home without these.

- **Credit card.** You might decide to fly to Vegas in order to extend your evening, in which case you'll need a few more outfits to look fabulous in, plus new underthings and essential toiletries to keep you feeling personally hygienic.

FIX-ITS ON THE FLY

Some things don't go exactly as you've planned. Here's how to keep the night afloat.

STAINS

Virtually any party-related stain—including spaghetti sauce—can be removed with club soda and hand soap. The only exception is red wine stains, which are best removed with white wine and soap. In each case, take a towel or a linen napkin (no paper products, please), soak the end in club soda or white wine, and dab vigorously at the stain. When it has faded significantly, rub a little hand soap on the wet towel and dab again. Later, it will launder beautifully.

FALLEN HEMS

Black electrical tape is the choice of professionals, but Scotch transparent tape will do in a pinch. Duct tape is okay for suits and blazers, but avoid using it on sheer or delicate fabrics.

BROKEN HEELS

If one heel breaks, you can remove the other—sometimes. Often, there are little nails sticking out that effectively turn your shoes into cleats. Although fine on the golf course, this is neither attractive nor comfortable in other situations. If just the lift has fallen

off (that little rubber cap at the bottom of your heel),
go to a corner store and buy a dried fruit roll-up.
Unroll the fruit, stand on one or two layers, and cut it
around the shape of your heel. The fruit leather will
become impaled on the nails and stay put for at least
a few hours—as long as you're not doing a lot of walk-
ing and it isn't extremely hot outside.

UMBRELLA EMERGENCY
Caught in an unexpected downpour? Cover your fine
self with a garbage bag, a newspaper, an inverted
shopping bag, or a broken umbrella plucked from the
nearest public trash can.

BROKEN FINGERNAIL
If you don't have your trusty tube of super glue with
you, take a piece of Scotch transparent tape and trim
it to the exact shape of your nail. It will keep that
wayward tip in place until you get home.

BROKEN EYEGLASS STEM
Break the plastic top off a push pin and insert the
pin through the screw hole between the stem and
the frame.

INSECT BITES
Apply dissolved Alka-Seltzer antacid, a paste of
baking soda, or a bit of Thousand Island dressing,
or swipe the bite with face powder from a compact.

RAZOR NICKS
All the best old-guy pharmacies sell styptic pencils.
They'll stop the bleeding immediately, so you can
wear that immaculate white shirt with confidence.

MUDDY SHOES
Remove dried mud with a paper towel or a brush (if you can get your hands on one). Then polish with petroleum jelly, moisturizer, shaving cream, whipped cream, milk, or—lucky you—shoe polish.

SUNBURN/WINDBURN
Slather your skin with mayonnaise or vinegar, or dab the burned area with a wet tea bag.

JELLYFISH STINGS
Splash the sting (not Sting) with vodka.

HOW TO BE A GOOD DATE

- Have a clear, agreed-upon plan that both parties are happy with.

- Don't be late. If it can't be helped, call well in advance and give a realistic ETA.

- If it's your first date, take separate cars (or public transportation) in case you need to escape.

- Kick the conversation football back and forth. If you feel like you're dominating the conversation, you probably are; switch sides and ask about your date's childhood, job, favorite vacation spots, and so on.

- Keep it light. On the first few dates you don't want to delve into your mother's psychological torture of you, your ex-spouse's trespasses, or the details of your chronic fungal infections.

WOMEN

- Dress well but not provocatively. If you really like the guy, wear "touchable" fabrics like cashmere or angora.

- Don't wear heels that make you tower over your date.

- Only insist on paying half if you never want to see the guy again.

MEN

- Make sure your car is clean if you're picking her up. You don't have to drive a Ferrari, but she shouldn't have to kick old McDonald's bags out of the way to find a place to plant her feet.

- Wear your best gear. It's much better to be over-dressed than underdressed. And anyway, dressing up is a sign of respect.

- Be a gentleman. Open doors, fetch coats, carry bags. And keep your conversation clean. You'd be amazed at how many women are offended when men swear or tell off-color jokes in front of them.

- Pay. Assuming you arranged the date, don't even think about letting her split the check or cover the tip. That can be a brush-off, didn't you know?

- Don't keep her out past her bedtime . . . at least for the first two or three dates. Like vaudevillians, good dates always leave 'em wanting more.

- Don't be pushy in the make-out department. A quick kiss on the lips is fine after a good first date, and a short-term make-out on the doorstep is fine after the second. After that you're on your own, but be sensitive to her verbal and physical clues.

FOUR THINGS TO DO ON A BLIND DATE

Many challenges are laid at the feet of the single man or woman. One of the most daunting is what to do and where to go with a person you've never met. Though the following suggestions aren't guaranteed to create magical chemistry, they're at least safe and somewhat wholesome.

BOWLING

Go ahead, laugh. But remember that bowling is one of the few sports that allows you to drink and smoke while you're doing it, and doesn't make you sweat. If you choose this option, find an out-of-the-way bowling alley with an excellent jukebox, and be prepared to consume hot dogs, chips, and pitchers of cheap beer. Also be prepared to study your date's backside every four minutes.

SHORT BOAT CRUISES

Perhaps your city offers a 3-hour twilight boat cruise down a scenic river, or your harbor has an evening-long "cruise to nowhere," with live music and cocktails. Excursions such as these provide a perfect opportunity to get to know someone. They also have the advantage of a predetermined docking time, in case you're anxious to call it a night.

CARNIVALS

It's very junior high, don't you think? And yet, carnivals are an excellent choice for blind dates because they offer the opportunity to impress her (if you're a man) by winning stuffed animals; to make him feel macho (if you're a woman) by screaming your head off on the roller coaster; and to get home in time (if the date's a bust) to call your friends and convince them to meet you for drinks.

OUTDOOR CONCERTS

Assuming you have similar tastes in music, an outdoor concert is an ideal place for two simpatico souls to come together. The superior nest-maker can roll out blankets on the grass, set up sand chairs, and light a lantern when the stars come out, while the better cook can spread out a picnic of delicacies (including sparkling wine, one hopes) to be consumed at a leisurely rate. At outdoor concerts, nobody minds if you talk during the show. Laughing and kissing are okay, too.

HOW TO GRACEFULLY DITCH A BAD DATE

Oh dear. Things aren't quite as delightful as you'd hoped for? Then it's time to call it a night (even if it's eight o'clock) and get on with your life. The problem with ditching bad dates is that, even though you desperately need to escape, you don't want to hurt anyone's feelings in the process. If you've read "How to Be a Good Date" (page 59), you will already have your own getaway car. With that in mind, here are a few useful strategies:

- Become ill. "I don't feel well . . . I think I might be having a reaction to the food/wine." It's a fine excuse, even if you're actually having a reaction to the company. Go home and live to date another day.

- Sneak off and call a friend. This only works if you have a cell phone. In the rest room, call the closest friend you can find and instruct him or her to call you back in 10 minutes with some kind of emergency. Choose the emergency carefully; you don't want to announce that your father's in the hospital or that your dog is dead, in case you have to back up these claims at a later date. Instead, say that there's a crisis "in the family" (don't say what) or "at work" (this is most effective if you're a journalist and there's breaking news, or you're a building superintendent and somebody's toilet has exploded). Make your apologies, pay the check (if you made the date), and run off into the night.

- Come right out and say it's not working. This doesn't have to be hurtful. You can point out the obvious, e.g., "I'm a Democrat, and you're a Republican. I'm allergic to cats and you have three. I'm a media junkie and you haven't watched TV since 1982. I think you're a wonderful person, but it doesn't seem like we have much of a future, does it?" Say thank you, pay the check (if you made the date), and run off into the night.

- Don't say you'll call if you have no intention of ever speaking to your date again. That only makes matters worse. Just say, "I'm glad we had the chance to meet," and leave it at that.

A woman of our acquaintance was having drinks in a restaurant with a blind date. The man excused himself to put money in the parking meter and never came back. She was not so much hurt as angry, bless her soul: she hunted him down, found him the next day at work, and made him apologize to her in front of everybody. He was hugely embarrassed. Serves him right.

CHAPTER 6

Savoir Faire

THE SOPHISTICATE'S GUIDE TO TIPPING

True savoir faire is nowhere more apparent than when one promptly, assuredly leaves an appropriate tip. *Hint*: Always carry $10 to $20 in small bills.

IN A RESTAURANT

WAITPERSON
Experts say that 15 percent is standard for good service. But 20 percent is nicer, and it's way easier to do the math—just double the first two digits of the check, like so:

total bill: $7.10	tip: $1.42
total bill: $48.23	tip: $9.60
total bill: $130.54	tip: $26
total bill: $273.42	tip: $54

Exception to the rule: Never leave less than $1, even if you've only had an egg sandwich and a cup of tea and your bill came to $4.

WINE STEWARD
Fifteen to 20 percent of the price of the bottle(s) you've ordered is standard—that is, if the steward has personally helped you. Otherwise, your server will probably take care of the steward at the end of the night.

PARKING VALET
Anywhere from $3 to $10 is acceptable, to be paid when your car is safely delivered to you—not before.

COAT CHECK

Again, this is paid when you pick up your coat. Tip $2 to $3 per item (hat, umbrella, etc.), unless you're in a really fancy joint. In that case, make it $5.

IN A BAR

If you're running a tab, the 20 percent rule stays steady.

If you're paying cash, it's a buck a drink for your bartender or cocktail server.

IN A HOTEL

PORTER OR BELL-PERSON

Three dollars per piece of luggage that he or she carries, amounting to no less than $5.

HOUSEKEEPING STAFF

Three to $5 per day. Again, leave no less than $5, and place it in an envelope in the room when you're ready to check out. If you've made a horrible mess, leave more. Lots more.

CONCIERGE

If he or she has made restaurant reservations, given you excellent directions, and so forth, tip him or her $10. If the concierge has scored you tickets to a sold-out Broadway show, or something nearly as heroic, make it $20.

ROOM SERVICE

Most hotels include an automatic 15 to 20 percent gratuity to the room service bill. It is not necessary, but certainly appreciated, to tip 15 percent in addition to the room charge.

IN A TAXI OR LIMO

TAXI
When you're buzzing around town, leave 15 to 20 percent of the fare, rounded off to the more generous dollar. Again, don't leave less than $1 no matter what. For rides to the airport, leave about 15 percent plus an extra dollar for each piece of luggage your driver hauls in and out of the trunk.

A NOTE TO THE SUAVE

You aren't the only one who has discovered, after hailing a cab, that you're riding around with no cash. Don't worry: just ask your cabbie to stop at a cash machine and wait while you refuel your wallet. It happens all the time.

PRIVATE LIMOUSINE OR CAR SERVICE
If the "limousine" is actually a minibus you're sharing to the airport, tip the driver for whatever bags he or she has carried for you. If it's an actual limousine that you've hired for a night on the town, a 20 percent tip is appropriate.

AT THE AIRPORT

SKYCAP OR PORTER
The standard $1 per bag rule applies to skycaps, but a full cart of luggage requires a $3 to $5 tip. When traveling with children or the elderly, you can often enlist a porter to help you and yours to the gate—in which case a $10 tip is due.

THE ART OF NEGOTIATION

IDLE LIMOUSINES

It's freezing outside, there are no cabs to be had, and there's a limo at the curb. The driver's reading a newspaper. Should you approach him? Of course! Limos and car services are often hired to wait for hours and hours outside restaurants, clubs, or events centers, while their "fares" frolic inside. Ask the driver if you can give him $10 to take you where you're going, assuming it's not too far away. If that doesn't do it, try $20. You'd be amazed at how often this works, and how much fun it can be. (See "Party-Crashing 101," page 50, for other limo uses.)

TICKET BROKERS

Please don't use the phrase "ticket scalper." It's considered by native Americans to be an ethnic slur. With that said, here's how to negotiate with those people who sell tickets on the street in front of sold-out events.

First of all, ticket resale is a supply-and-demand business. Ticket brokers sometimes offer huge discounts. Depending on the event, you might be able to buy tickets on the street for $20 that cost $60 at the box office. A broker who has overbought would rather get $10 than no dollars for the piece of cardboard he's holding. So when you approach a ticket broker, consider these elements: 1) If the event is sold out, the tickets will be significantly marked up. In a major city, expect a 100 to 300 percent markup; in the boonies, you can probably get tickets for 50 percent more than the printed price. 2) Seats in the first couple of rows are at a premium. 3) If the event is woefully underattended, offer 60 or 70 percent off the printed ticket price and haggle up from there.

4) Remember that street sales on the day of the event are the ticket broker's last chance to make a buck. If he or she is unloading tickets a half hour before the event, you're at a huge advantage—so take advantage.

RETAIL HAGGLING

This can be done more often than you think. You've haggled with people selling umbrellas and scarves on the street, right? Most small stores that are having a sale or a clearance are open to haggling—if you can deal directly with the owner. Consider the tale of a friend who was eyeballing a $299 lamp (originally $500) at an end-of-season sale. He spoke to the shop's owner about lowering the price, and the owner said to come back the next day. The friend returned, the lamp was still there, and he walked away with it for $100—including tax. Prices of furniture, cars, services, airline tickets, hotel rooms and now, thanks to the Internet, even groceries are open to friendly discussion.

A NOTE TO THE SUAVE

Before driving away with that rental car or settling that hotel room bill, ask the clerk (or better yet, the manager) if there are discounts for using a particular credit card, corporate discounts, club member discounts, or student/senior discounts.

THE ONLY BAR (OR PARLOR) TRICKS YOU'LL EVER NEED

THE TELEPATHIC COIN

Get an assortment of four or five distinctly different coins—quarter, dime, nickel, bright penny, dull penny, etc. Put them in a hat, if you've got one. A dry glass or clean ashtray will also work. Turn away and ask your pal to pick a coin and place it against his or her forehead for a few seconds, so that the coin will be infused with special vibes. When the coin has been returned to the hat, feel around for the warmest one, and produce it with a flourish. Voilà! You're a genius!

THE TWO-TON BOX OF MATCHES

For this classic trick you'll need a box of matches and a pack of cigarettes. Place the cigarette pack on its side (on top of the Surgeon General's warning), and put the matches on the table at the base of the pack. Invite your victim to put the box of matches on top of the cigarette pack—using only the first finger and ring finger, while keeping the middle finger on the table at all times. No fair using the thumb or any other digits for assistance. Unless your victim is a yoga master, it will be very difficult to lift the pack more than an inch. The secret trick is to extend the middle finger first, then tilt your hand forward. Even then, it isn't easy. Practice at home first, especially if you're betting that *you* can do it.

THE OLIVE TRICK

Here's the challenge—how do you get an olive in an upside-down glass into a second glass that is right side up? It sounds easy until you learn the rules: your hand cannot touch the olive, and you cannot use the side of a table to slide the olive from one glass to another. Tricky, but here's how it's done.

Place a very round olive underneath a glass on a flat surface, such as (you guessed it) a bar. Move the glass so that the olive begins to circle the inside of the glass. Increase this circular motion and the momentum of the spinning glass will lift the olive up off of the flat surface. Still swirling the glass, lift it and the olive up and quickly place a second glass, right side up, below the first glass. When you stop moving the first glass, the olive drops into the second.

MAKE A MATCH CHANGE COLOR

This trick requires a matchbook in which the matches have a color—let's say white—on one side and the cardboard's natural gray color on the back. Pull two matches out of a matchbook, and hold them by their heads between your thumb and forefinger, so that the sticks of the matches rise vertically from your hand. Show your audience the gray side. Then turn your hand toward your chest, and while doing so nimbly turn the match heads between your thumb and forefinger. Then show the audience that the "other side" is also gray. Your audience now thinks that your matchsticks are all one color. Bounce your hand on a table or flat surface while turning the match heads again, so that the white sides show. Congratulations, you have now turned the cardboard white—at least that's what your unwitting audience will think.

THE ONLY JOKE YOU'LL EVER NEED

Two guys are sitting at a bar. One says to the other, "Where are you from?" Guy answers, "Ireland." The first guy says, "No kidding! Me too! Let's have a round to celebrate." They drink a shot and guy #2 says, "I grew up in Dublin, how about you?" Guy #1 is overjoyed: "I grew up in Dublin, too! That calls for

another shot!" "Church?" "St. Mary's." "Me too!"
"Birthday?" "September 25th." "I don't believe it!
That's my birthday, too!" By this time the drinks are
really flying, and someone at the other side of the bar
asks the bartender what's going on. The bartender
says, "Oh, the O'Malley twins are at it again."

FOUR DANCE STEPS YOU'LL NEED TO KNOW

1. Box step

2. Waltz

3. Swing

4. Two-step

FOUR ADVANCED STEPS THAT ARE FUN TO KNOW

1. Fox-trot

2. Cha-cha

3. Tango

4. Macarena

We don't expect you to attend advanced ballroom
courses to learn this stuff. Just spend an evening or
two with the best dancer you know, in the privacy of
a secure living room, and get the basics down so you
can confidently slow-dance with your Uncle Frank at
your cousin's wedding and also hold your own in
ballrooms and gin mills from Malibu to Monte
Carlo—and everywhere in between.

CLASSIC GAMES FOR A SOCIAL LIFETIME

From backyards to country clubs, summer beach houses to casinos, knowing a few games can provide amusement and connections with friends, strangers, even children. How many of these 65 classic games are in your repertoire?

Card games: bridge, canasta, crazy eights, cribbage, gin rummy, hearts, pinochle, poker, setback

Board games: backgammon, checkers, chess, Chinese checkers, dominos, go, mah jongg, mancala

Casino games: baccarat, bingo, blackjack, craps, keno, pai gow, roulette

Bar games: boss dice, darts, liar's dice, poker dice, pool, quarters, shuffleboard

Athletic challenges: bowling, croquet, golf, horseshoes, table tennis, softball, tennis, volleyball

The weekend guest or host will often find him or herself in the company of children. You probably remember most, if not all, of these childhood favorites, and it never hurts to make yourself useful by entertaining the smallest guests.

Children's games: charades, dodgeball, duck duck goose, go fish, hangman, hide and seek, hopscotch, hot potato, jacks, jump rope, marbles, Marco Polo, memory, Mother may I, musical chairs, old maid, pick-up sticks, pin the tail on the donkey, red light/green light, red rover, rocks paper scissors, tag, telephone, tic-tac-toe, truth or dare, war

ESSENTIAL FRENCH
PARLEZ-VOUS PAR-TAY?

It's almost impossible to have fun—in this or any other country—without knowing a few key French words and phrases. Memorize the following:

à la carte (ah lah KAHRT): Literally "from the card," it refers to a menu in which everything is sold individually, i.e., no automatic salad or vegetables with dinner.

apéritif (ah-pehr-uh-TEEF): A light drink, such as champagne or sherry, served before a meal as an alleged appetite stimulant.

Armagnac (ar-mahn-YAK): A French brandy similar to cognac, but made in a different region.

au naturel (oh nahtoo-REHL): In France it means, "prepared in its natural state," i.e., raw. In the United States and the United Kingdom it means nude, unclothed, in the buff, or buck naked.

au revoir (oh reh-VWAHR): Good-bye; literally, "see you again."

à votre santé (ah VOH-truh SAHN-tay): "To your health," a classic French toast (not of the breakfast food variety).

beau geste (boh ZHEST): A grand and beautiful gesture, such as picking up the tab at your table of 12.

beau monde (boh MOHND): Fashionable society. Though it literally means "beautiful world," it refers to people, not geography.

bel esprit (behl eh-SPREE): Wit combined with elegance.

blanc de blanc (BLAHNGK duh BLAHNGK): White wine or champagne made entirely from white grapes.

blanc de noir (BLAHNGK duh NWAHR): White (or pink) wine or champagne made from red (black) grapes.

bon soir (bohn SWAHR): Good night; good-bye.

bon vivant (bohn vee-VAH): A person who likes the finer things in life such as good food, drink, music, art, literature, and parties.

brut (BROOT): Very dry. See CHAMPAGNE.

canapés (KAN-uh-pay): Small pieces of bread or crackers topped with garnishes or cheese and served as an appetizer, usually with cocktails.

champagne (sham-PAYN): Technically, a sparkling wine made in the Champagne region of France. Though several U.S. winemakers ignore French customs and call their sparkling wine champagne, in other regions of the world it's called *Cava* (Spain), *Sekt* (Germany), and *Spumante* (Italy).

Châteaubriand (sha-toh-bree-AHN): Not a kind of wine, but a beef dish, usually large enough for two.

chez (SHAY): At the home of, as in, "Come for a soirée at 8 P.M., *chez* Smith."

coupe (KOOP): The traditional, birdbath-shaped champagne glass, said to have originally been fashioned to fit one of Marie Antoinette's breasts.

débonnaire (DAY-boh-nayr): Though it means "good-natured and easy-going," it also suggests a person who is comfortable in any social gathering.

décolletage (day-koh-leh-TAHZH): A low-cut neckline.

demi-monde (DUH-mee-MOHND): A class of women on the fringes of respectable society. See DÉCOLLETAGE.

digestif (dee-zheh-STEEF): A spirit such as brandy or cognac consumed after dinner, as a so-called aid to digestion.

garçon (gar-SOHN): Boy. *Not* "waiter," unless you want to be snubbed in restaurants for the rest of your life.

gourmand (goor-MAHND): One who appreciates gourmet food to an excessive degree.

gourmet (goor-MAY): One who appreciates fine food; also refers to high-quality, artfully presented food.

hors d'oeuvres (or DERV): Small appetizers served before a meal. The singular and the plural forms are pronounced the same way, in case you're trying to win a bet.

joie de vivre (ZHWAH duh VEEV'r): Joy of life.

l'addition (LAH dee-syon): The check.

liqueur (lih-KUHR): A sweet alcoholic drink such as Grand Marnier, Pernod, or Sambuca, usually served after dinner.

méthode champenoise (may-TOHD shahm-peh-NWAHZ): Quality sparkling wine, fermented in the bottle, not in a tank as big as your house.

prix fixe (pree FEEX): Fixed price. Usually refers to a kind of package-deal menu in which courses, from appetizers to dessert, are preselected and sold for a single price.

rendezvous (ron-DAY-voo): An engagement or date.

RSVP: Short for "répondez s'il vous plaît," meaning, "please reply." If you ignore your RSVP duties, you may be considered *déclassé* (fallen in social standing).

savoir faire (SAH-vwahr FAYR): Literally "knowing how to do," it's a quality of having finely tuned social graces.

s'il vous plaît (seel voo PLAY): Please.

soirée (swa-RAY): An evening party.

suave (SWAHV) *Larousse* says it means "sweet and agreeable," but in the U.S. it means smooth, in a worldly sort of way.

THE FREIXENET STORY

Freixenet is a family company that was started with a marriage in Barcelona, Spain, over a century ago. Today, the family still lives above the winery, and, with much good fortune, Freixenet has become the world's largest producer of sparkling wines. Our *méthode champenoise* wines are recommended by wine critics the world over.

CORDON NEGRO BRUT

This is the best-selling imported sparkling wine in America. *USA Today* calls it "a truly remarkable sparkler for the money." It comes in the striking black frosted bottle, dressed for special events. A true brut, it is crisp, clean, very dry, and smooth.

CORDON NEGRO EXTRA DRY

Also in the black frosted bottle, this wine is somewhat fruitier than our Brut, with a refreshing, slightly fuller taste. Perfect for those who consider our Brut too dry. Look for the gold star.

CORDON NEGRO ESTATE

This special cuvée in the fat, black frosted bottle is our winemaker's epitome of balance and finesse. Only the first pressings of the finest grapes in our purview are good enough. Hard to find, though!

CARTA NEVADA BRUT AND SEMI-SECO

Easily recognizable by its distinctive nontinted frosted bottle and gold label, Carta Nevada is low in acidity with a soft, full taste that makes it the perfect wine to serve at dinner events or brunches, with flavorful or spicy dishes, or as a mixer in punches and champagne cocktails. The Brut is crisp and dry; the Semi-Seco is semidry.

SPUMANTE

Soon to be regarded as the premier spumante, Freixenet Spumante is attractively packaged in a distinctive white frosted bottle. Made in the time-honored traditional champagne method, it has a taste that is smoothed by time, not by added sugar. Its light, refreshing taste goes quite well with pastries and fruit, at brunches or weddings, or any event that calls for spumante.

BRUT DE NOIRS

This salmon-pink sparkler is surprisingly dry and lively, combining the soft fruitiness reminiscent of a quality merlot with the sophistication of a prestige champagne. Some say pink sparklers are the most romantic of all.

BRUT NATURE

This is our top cuvée, aged for five full years. It is delicate, bone dry, and many critics say it is our finest wine. Brut Nature is a cuvée made of reserve wines from those years when a vintage is proclaimed. Only a limited number of cases of this sparkler in its green frosted bottle are produced.

Méthode Champenoise—CAVA—